D0862023

Searching
for God
and Finding *the*
Treasure

A woman's life long search for God and her discovery that
God may be found in unexpected places.
God may be the God of surprises.

Enjoy - and don't
give up on finding
the TREASURE !
S. Sandra

SISTER SANDRA MAKOWSKI SSMN, JCL

Searching for God and Finding the Treasure

Copyright © 2022 by Sister Sandra Makowski SSMN, JCL.

Published by Pen Culture Solutions   08/31/2022

Pen Culture Solutions
1-888-727-7204 (USA)
1-800-950-458 (Australia)
support@penculturesolutions.com

Contents

Foreword

Searching for God can be a journey of revelation as well as a journey of faith. It can be an uphill hike through miles of forests and fields of blossoms and color and glory—but also filled with surprise, disappointment, doubt and discovery.

The following story is a story of one woman's search for God. This woman, the seeker, recounts to the reader, her search and her discovery of who God is for her. There are many parts of her life story which is not told in this book—but this book does offer the reader the significant moments in the seeker's life where she felt compelled, by life experiences, to stop, remember, recount, and reflect on where and who God is and has been for her. Her life has been and still is filled with moments of God's glory revealed to her through people, places and graces—but the journey also led to many surprises along the way.

This seeker chooses to recount not only her moments of joy and discovery, but also her moments of doubt, disorder and upheaval and finally her moments of finding God in the search.

Why does this seeker choose to recount her moments of doubt, her moments of grace and her moments of feeling invisible? Because these experiences are all a part of her journey in her search for God, And it was through these moments that became grace-filled that she found God in unexpected places and people. God is a God of surprise. Where you expect to find God you may be surprised, and where you don't expect to find God you may also be surprised. This is her message in writing her story - that the reader may come to realize that God is there for you in all your moments of life—but, also that God is a God of surprise. As this poem states; "For the Lord will never leave you—nor will any true friend. God's true love will shine upon you, right to the very end. And again, don't be surprised, when this will lead to something beautiful right before your very eyes."

Where we stand, we stand alone.
Not on a pedestal of silver and gold
But more on something unsteady and cold.

No one in front of me no one behind

No one to carry on the pleasures that bind.

But I hear the voice of God who speaks to me as my true friend
God says my love with shine upon you right to the very end.

I'm the last one, I'm by myself
Looking around, but nobody is there.

Feeling abandoned and no one to care.
Find me a purpose a reason to be
Freedom from loneliness and freedom to see

That life has a vision, a purpose and a prize
That will lead to something beautiful
It should be no surprise.

The prize that will be, will be beautiful to see.
It will reveal that the unsteady and cold
Is really filled with silver and gold.

And people you have met on your path throughout your life
Are there to stand with no throughout all your strife.
You are really not alone.
Choirs of angels singing this all in one accord.

That if you feel lost than turn to the Lord..

And again, don't be surprised
That this will lead to something beautiful
Right before your very eyes.

And I hear the voice of God who speaks to me as my true friend
God says my love with shine upon you right to the very end.

Introduction

All the passengers were safely settled in their seats with their seat belts securely fastened, and the plane took off on schedule. Anticipating a calm and un-eventful one hour flight, she silently recited her 'safe flight' prayer—asking God to protect and guide the plane safely to its destination.

On this airline she had a window seat which is usually what she requested, and it did not take long for the plane to ascend into the sky and begin sailing through the clouds. And, she found herself again, as she did often before, searching through the maze of clouds. Her eyes scanned the cirrus clouds which appeared as wispy streaks in the sky. They seem to form a line of feathers reaching out beyond what one can see. Next came the clouds that reminded her of cotton balls in the sky. And finally, the lowest level of clouds - stratus clouds that cover the sky like bed sheets or huge gray blankets that hang low in the sky. And, she continued her search, and she continued her prayer.

As she gazed out the airplane window she asked God the big question. *"Where are you God? Are you hiding in the clouds? If one cloud disappeared quickly in the sky, would I find you behind that hidden cloud, sitting on a throne like sky-king perhaps? At a distance the clouds appeared to form an outline of a face—could that be you O God? Have you been hiding all along—are you playing hide and seek with me? Where are you? Since I don't know what you look like would I even recognize you if you revealed yourself to me?* "A life of searching and struggle and unending questions regarding faith, discipleship, and the presence of God— that's what follows her now- the questions—the never ending questions—like—*"where are you? Have we already met -you and me- and maybe I didn't recognize you—that's the scary part—were you the neighbor next door? Are you the passenger sitting next to me on this plane? Or, do I see you when I look in the mirror? Has my life been filled with your presence but I was too busy to notice, since I was always looking somewhere else? Maybe you are right in front of me —the divine in my midst. Please show me a sign O God, that you never left my side."*

So—again—in her forever search for God… this becomes her prayer. *"Speak to the seekers O God—those who have sought your face in the journey of life and tell us—where you are. Help all to see and recognize you in the stillness of our hearts."*

A HEART IN SEARCH

Could you, O God, be found in the search?
In the unexpected sounds, or
places, or spaces, or faces?

Could you be in the neighbor who
lives with mules and horses?
Or
The woman who's condemned by the
church because of her two divorces?

Could you be found in the movement of grace,
like a petal falling off a flower or a smile on a face?

Could you, O God be in the
sound of a bird call,
Or
the beauty of a colored leaf,
Or
the sun breaking through the trees
in the soft gentle breeze?

Could you be in the color of spring or fall?
In the writer's pen, and
The artists' brush, and
The worker's fatigue, and
The afternoon quiet, and
The slow pace of a moment of grace?

Could you O God be in the search?
Are you just calling me to look even deeper?

Or are you just saying to me "just open
your eyes because I'm right here"?

Or, "Listen to the sound of my voice—I am calling you by name."?

THUS BEGINS THE SEARCH

THE LIFETIME SEARCH FOR GOD

Chapter One

BEGINNING THE SEARCH

She walked slowly to her office—one brave foot in front of the other and she sat down at her desk. The lights in the room switched on automatically. Darkness takes leave, and makes room for a spark of light searching for entrance.

She makes the sign of the cross.

She pauses to recount her experiences where she thought she had lost sight of God and realizes now that it was not up to her to determine where God was or wasn't. She kept up the search.

She turns on her tired, weary self–the voice, the smile, the persona that she worked so hard to embrace. With years of schooling and years of service in the church, she enters into the world of her memories. She recalls the people whom she has met, the men and women who have suffered and triumphed in giving their lives to God in the service of the church. She recalls their journey –their experiences of doubt and fear, and, in the end, enlightened and finding peace through their intense struggle of faith.

She begins by asking the following questions:

Did you grow up Catholic, and did you receive all of your sacraments and attend Catholic school? And did you help Sister clean up the classroom after school and then help carry her book bag to the convent? And, did she give you a scapular to wear as a present for helping her? That surely felt good since it assured you of freedom from Satan and a happy death. Then, as you got older, did you join a catholic youth group? Then, later in life, did you become a CCD teacher or help in a confirmation class? Your faith, your church, your catholic schooling was and may still remain a part of who you are as a Christian, as a good Catholic. It defined you.

But, lately has your faith been tested? With all that has been revealed lately with regard to sexual abuse scandals, the lifestyle occurring in many seminaries and the cover-ups of scandal by priests, bishops and cardinals, this may lead to a crisis of faith. Was all of this happening in the one, holy, Catholic and apostolic church which, you were taught, would bring salvation? What is going on? You've most likely heard the expression 'a crisis of faith'? Is that what is happening? And, has this crisis of faith led you to re-examine some of your life experiences and even to question the presence of God?

This may sound depressing, and maybe it is. But, the search for God could be an adventure—you might even discover that God is in the search. God is in the unexpected places and people.

She begins the following narrative as a seeker—as one who grew up Catholic and attended catholic school. And, some of what you read may relate to your own story as well. Maybe you also received your sacraments, obeyed someone whom you considered holy, and perhaps you worked for many years for and in the church. Many experiences may have led to beauty and wonder, but perhaps many also have led you to doubt, anger, and a deeper search for God. God was there—in the moment, in the experience, but in the unexpected place—God was in the search.

This seeker of God then discovered that her life –long vocation was to be a religious Sister. Many of her experiences recount what it was like, after Vatican Council II and after the Code of Canon Law took effect in 1983, when Catholic Sisters worked in parishes, schools, and administrative offices. Many of their experiences led them to meet the People of God in the most needed areas of service. They met the true servants of God in those who served the poor and the most vulnerable. They met these servants in the pews and in the eyes and ears of the priestly servants of God on the altar. But, also, in many instances, they also discovered that some things don't change–in many instances she and the Catholic Sisters she knew, in many instances, were treated as servants and slaves of the church hierarchy. Clericalism was alive and well.

Many of these stories burst open the presumption that one will find God in places and people considered sacred and holy, and, for the better part of one's life, this may be the case. But, many of these stories also will remind us that we cannot take that for granted. God may not always be visible in the most expected people or places. Some of these stories can leave us feeling skeptical and scared, and even angry. Because if God isn't where we were taught God would be–and in what we were taught as sacred and holy–then, where is God? These stories follow that question with great longing–because a face, an act of kindness, a moment of forgiveness or grace led this seeker to find God and God's face in the surprise of the divine.

Every stone on the road is precious, and sometimes the road of life appears long and dangerous, as well as winding and cruel. But the road can also be a voyage of virtue and one can learn from this struggle that we call life.

Let us now enter into this seeker's story.

Chapter Two

LOOKING FOR GOD IN TODAY'S CHURCH

"The only one who can teach me to find God, is God alone." - Thomas Merton

"God is not restricted to the Sabbath's dawn, to 11 a.m. on Sundays, and in certain buildings we have set aside for God. God is where we are. And where we are not. All the time. No exceptions. We can expect to be surprised by God." Thomas Merton

It all began when she was just eight years of age ...

A. GROWING UP CATHOLIC

GRADE SCHOOL–HER FIRST CONFESSION

She was just eight years old–a happy, carefree young girl, who loved to play the piano and sing in the school choir. The first book she ever read, from cover to cover, was a book about St. Joan of Arc. She thought it would be a great accomplishment to become a saint, and she was hoping that maybe someday she could become one, although being burned at the stake was not quite her cup of tea. She hoped to find an easier way to sainthood.

She was learning about the sacraments–thus began her search for God, although she did not know it at the time. All she knew was that she was preparing to make her first confession. It spooked her out quite a bit–she didn't like being cramped into the small space called the confessional. But, she practiced long and hard, and, with the help of Sr. St. Theresa, she learned the proper

words and the proper formula. With a lot of practice she would overcome her nervousness and make Jesus happy.

She stood in line, with her hands folded, and kept quietly reciting what she was going to say once she entered the confessional, which she named the little black cell. However, when the time actually came she remembered her memorized sins, but she forgot the words: "I am sorry for these sins and all the sins of my past life." These words were to let the confessor know that she was finished. That is what Sister taught her. But she had a hard enough time remembering what her sins were, much less the words to end her confession. So—when finishing the list of memorized sins, she ended her confession by saying "and, Father, that's all." She was so nervous and frightened, in that little black cell, that she hoped Father could guide her through this, her first confession. Well, Father did no such thing. In fact, he gave her orders to leave the confessional, would not give her absolution, told her to go back to Sister and ask her how she is supposed to end her confession, then, get back in line, and try all over again. She did what she was told, but it was a long time before she made her second confession.

It was only years later, when she found herself teaching the sacraments to middle grade school children that her first confession was brought to the surface of her memory. She kept wondering later if the feelings she felt after that confession was what grace is supposed to feel like. She was told that she would receive grace when receiving a sacrament. The only thing she felt she received was the feeling of failure, and fear, and a great sigh of relief when it was over.

The Baltimore catechism, for those who are familiar with it, gives the definition of a sacrament as an outward sign, instituted by Christ, to give grace. One was taught that you would find Jesus by receiving the sacraments of the church, and she realizes now that she never forgot her feelings of shame and fear and wondered how God was present to her at that most unforgettable moment.

I confessed my sins to Father that day.

He told me what to do and he told me what to pray.

I made the sign of the cross with fear
Because Father told me that the devil was near.

I began to be afraid being in that little black cell.
I began to believe that I was going to hell.

Is that what it's like to have God so near?
Yet each time I confessed, all I felt was fear.

The Seeker asked herself these questions:

Where was God in this sacrament of the church—an outward sign instituted by Christ to give grace? That is what she was taught as the definition of a sacrament. Was this really a moment of grace, or more a moment of fear?

Are there many moments like this when we are caught by a surprising revelation–that God is not clearly visible to us in the way we might expect God to be? Could God be present through the sacrament, but clearly in an unexpected way?

"O my God, I am heartily sorry for having offended thee– and, I detest all my sins because of thy just punishment."

It was many years after this first confession that she realized that she had been reciting the word 'hardly sorry' instead of' heartily sorry ' and that the real reason that she 'detested' all her sins had a lot to do with the fear of punishment rather than 'because they offend thee my God."

But, the longer she pondered and prayed, she realized that this was an incredibly teachable moment.

She discovered that God did not let her down. She discovered throughout her life experiences that God would hear and heal her fears and carry her through the peace and serenity that this sacrament can bring–and that it only exists as a sacrament when it is an outward sign instituted by Christ to give grace. It will truly give grace, not fear and pettiness …but grace. God knows that she will recognize sin when it happens and when those moments in her life arrive, that God's love and forgiveness will be there to lead her.

But, will she someday also discover that this kind of God is with her no matter where she goes—that God was where she was, and no place, and no time of day, is a stranger to God's presence?

It was only later in life, I found deep in my heart
That I knew God and me would never be apart.

My prayer said it all, and God said it too.
Over and over, in the Bible: "I love you."
God continues to say "I know you'll be true.
So, don't ever doubt the love I have for you".

A pondering Heart

A sacrament, as defined by the church, is an outward sign instituted by Christ to give grace. When you reflect back on your first reception of the sacraments, what comes to your mind? Were they moments of grace, moments of fear, or both?

Was your experience of the reception of the sacraments totally different from what you thought it would be like? If so, in what way?

In your search for God, was God's strength and support given to you when you received a sacrament of the church, and/or did it lead you to a greater and deeper depth of God's presence?

MIDDLE SCHOOL–A HAPPY DAY

She grew to love the Sisters who taught her in grade school. She would help Sister Joseph Marie and carry her bookbag for her to the convent after school. She also began to take piano lessons at the convent once a week, and even though Sister Rosalia would fall asleep during her piano class she always came to full attention when her student hit a wrong note. Then, when she would spend extra time at the convent to practice the piano Sister Mary Agnes always seemed to show up with a glass of milk and a cookie which she thought went real well with piano practice. Those were days when she looks back now and knows full well that God was there. When the Sisters gathered together in their little chapel to sing what was called 'the divine office' she felt that heaven had fallen from the sky and filled the convent with God's glory. If there ever was a moment of stillness, of peace, and tranquility it was that time, and that place that filled her heart with peace. She didn't have to look for God–God was revealed in the atmosphere of caring, loving and service.

A Pondering heart

- Can you recall moments in your life where God was revealed to you through an atmosphere of caring, loving and service?

- Can you recall a time in your life where you would describe an experience as feeling like 'heaven falling from the sky"?

- If you were asked to imagine, in art, a heart filled with peace, what would your picture be?

HIGH SCHOOL–WHERE WAS GOD?

The drill was on–right was right and wrong was wrong. There is no middle road, no what ifs, no exception–not in this high school run by this Holy Order of Sisters. There is one way to heaven–follow the rules, obey your parents, say your prayers, keep the commandments. This was her high school teachers' rules-pray and obey. That is the road to heaven.

The students began their day in high school by meeting Sister Robertine at the door as she stood straight and stern, with her yard stick in hand. Before entering the school the girls had to get on their knees so that the length of their skirt could be measured. If it didn't touch the ground then they were in violation of the school's dress code, which led to demerits, detention, and then suspension. The Sisters were tough, emotionless, militaristic and very different from the Sisters who taught her in grade school.

She recalls her sophomore English assignment. The class was asked to write a short story that addressed the topic of telling a story of someone's day. She remembers writing a story of a little girl with a brown paper bag- who walked into Ed's grocery story on the corner of Court and Rutherford St.

I knew Ed the grocery man. That's what I called him. He had real kind eyes and big hands and he was always helping me when I tried to get the bubble gum out of the machine. He would give it a big knock with his knuckle and I always ended up with a few more pieces of gum than anyone else who

knocked on that machine. It was always good to have Ed on your side.

But this day was different. We had no food at home. It was another food-less night. I know my Mom was sad as was Sissy,

and, since I had no idea how to get money, I wondered if there was a way I could get food. The only way I could come up with was to borrow some food at Ed's grocery store. Maybe he might even give me some if I asked. But what if he said no? I couldn't take that chance. I will certainly pay him back some day when we had the money. But, I was still afraid - taking food without paying for it was not something I learned in school. But my Mom's tears and my sister's silent stare was also foreign and frightening to me. I had to act, courageously and boldly for their sake. So—I walked in one afternoon with a brown paper bag hidden under my jacket. When Ed was busy with a customer I quickly made the moves that I had rehearsed—down the cracker aisle, put some in the bag—quick - down the cereal aisle—put some in the bag—quick. Grabbed what I could real fast and said to Ed; "I'll be back. I forgot to get Mom's grocery list"—I waved good-bye real fast and took off, but Ed seemed very involved in a conversation with the bearded man which made me feel pretty confident that he didn't see me grabbing the crackers and mini cereal boxes as I fled the store. I had never done this before—but I tried to keep my mind on my Mom and Sis- otherwise I would have thrown up right on the street corner. Half way home I kept my mind on how this night would end. We had food—not much—but some. I started skipping with the brown paper bag over my shoulder and then I began to dance my way home - full of guilt, but also filled with glee, knowing that tonight's meal will be better than the night before.

Well—this was the English composition that she handed in to her teacher, Sister Anastasia—the story of the little girl with the brown paper bag. When read by Sister it did not go well at all. Sister called her to the front of the class, explained to her why she gave her a failing mark on her English assignment and told her, that by writing something so horrendous, she was encouraging acts of sinfulness. How could she possibly allow her pen to actually compose a story of someone who seemed so happy to have committed a sin? Shame on you—she said to her—is that what you are encouraging people to do- commit sin and then dance the rest of the way home?

Needless to say, she was shocked. She thought she wrote an A+ story for her English assignment - and here she was, being admonished for it. Wait just a minute, Sister! She wanted to shout—don't you know anything—have you no idea what this little girl went through—step in her shoes for a day and then tell me that she is a sinner!!! Anger welled up inside of her. After all, this was only an English assignment. She wrote about something that tempted her heart and her words into sympathy and compassion. And, again, this was a story, but it is possible that it could be a story that some could recognize as their own story. Why would Sister just toss her away in front of her classmates because she wrote a composition that could easily have been someone's desperate home situation? This was an

English assignment not spiritual direction. But, what did it matter now–she was certainly treated as a sinner in front to her classmates because of what she wrote.

A Pondering heart

- Was this little girl a sinner for what she wrote?

- Was God going to punish her for a freely written composition?

- Was God mad at her? And was Sister right all along–that this 'fictional' character who she wrote about was really a sinner?

- What kind of a God would that be? Is this the kind of God that we are called to believe in–the punishing God?

- How can this seeker discover anew the real God who loves her, whether she be a sinner or a saint?

- Who is the God whom we really long for–does this God love no matter what- does this God forgive, no matter what?

HIGH SCHOOL GRADUATION

Ah, here she is at last - recalling, very clearly, the day of her high-school graduation - the highly anticipated moment in every high schoolers list of unforgettable moments. Her's was unforgettable, but for a whole different reason. She remembers it well—there she was in line, garbed in her graduation gown and cap in her hand, ready to walk down the aisle in front of an auditorium of people—ready to receive her high school diploma—when suddenly she was approached by Sister Mary know-it-all who told her that her tuition was never paid. So, Sister pulled her out of line, and told her that she could not graduate. Here she was - the moment every senior waits for, with family and friends sitting in the front rows waiting to capture this wonderful moment. There was nothing else she could do but bawl like a baby. What was there left to do?

Now, the good news is that Sister had a momentary conversion, or else she didn't know what to do with a bawling wanna be high -school graduate. She ended up telling her that she would put a blank sheet of paper in the diploma case and she could go up and receive a 'pretend' diploma and, at least, save face in front of family and friends.

The rest of the day went as planned, a big graduation party at home, with almost no words spoken about the incident until 15 year later, when her mother met one of her former teachers at a nearby shopping mall. That teacher checked the old school records and discovered that the parish actually paid for her daughter's tuition, but it was never properly recorded in the school records. Good to know—but it sure as heck didn't make a difference 15 years later. The pain of that moment was already etched in her heart.

- Oh, the drama that hangs on these memories, drama that led to depression and confusion. She remembers being taught from the Baltimore catechism. She was taught that God was found in the church sacraments, in the church congregation and in the church's official leaders. But, in this very dramatic moment she did not recognize God. Was God really present?

A pondering heart

 Did you ever have an experience that was supposed to be a celebration, but instead became an unexpected experience of depression and confusion?

19

Was God present in that experience, but just not in the way you expected?

What was this seeker to learn from this experience - where was God leading her—and where was God in this journey?

- If God was not present in the fear, or the embarrassment, or the feeling of failure, where was God present?

- But where… Where was God?

The God of my Evermore

O God, if you were a color in the rainbow -
What color would you be?
And are you really larger than the ocean
and taller than the tallest tree?

And God, if you were a lover
How would your love be expressed?
In the grandeur of emotion, or
In the heart that needs a rest -
A rest from this world all drunk with evil
That spins this earth profound.
Please God express your love, and
spread it all around.

And God, if you were a poet
Would your words sing a song
Of love and truth and beauty
That would carry us along?

Would we be carried down a road
of words echoed from above?

If so, then God - please be that poet
And rhyme your words with love.

And God—if you were one of my neighbors
Would I be able to be true
To you O God, of love and mercy.
And, would I speak to them of you?
Or, have I passed you God, in the shadows and
Do I often forget your name?
Have I sometimes given up on me
And figured you would do the same?

O God, you may be a color, a poet, a
lover or my neighbor next door.
But please dear God I also implore
That you be my hero—the one I adore—
for you are the God of my evermore.

Chapter Three

꧁ ꧂

LOOKING FOR GOD AS A RELIGIOUS SISTER AND AS A WOMAN IN TODAY'S CHURCH

And so she continued her search–for holiness, for wholeness, for the meaning of life–for days in the shade– and for nights in warmth and wonder, and most of all, for God and who God was calling her to be.

She became a Sister–a Sister working for the church, working for the People of God. That was her understanding of how one would describe the church after Vatican Council II. She did not expect to meet the kind of church that she was soon introduced to in her ministry as a Sister. Certainly, and gratefully she met men and women devoted to the Word of God, who gave their lives in the service of God. But, surprisingly, she also met dysfunction on all levels, especially on the level of clericalism, which James Carroll describes as the root of Roman Catholic dysfunction. Vatican Council II brought the altar down from on high, on the level of the congregation. But the depth and breadth of clericalism raised it even higher than it was before the Council. What she discovers is not easy revelations, but hard truths–that God is not always where we expect God to be.

Ministry #1

She remembers her first years as a religious sister and her first job in church ministry. She looked forward to her first parish assignment. She will be serving God by serving people in the parish, and she will learn what pastoral ministry means from the pastor and priests assigned to the parish. She will learn service, self-giving, generosity, humility, and love of God's Word. This is where she will find God.

Did She?

She remembers her boss, Pastor Bob. He seldom had time to speak with her—at least he seldom made time. Her position in the parish was unclear, and seemed to depend on the mood that he was in. She approached Pastor Bob one day with a request for a luncheon meeting, away from the busy rectory, pastoral office, ringing phones and doorbells, so that some serious conversation could occur without interruption. He agreed. The restaurant was chosen, food ordered and eaten, conversation concluded, which, actually, led to nowhere. Now—both pairs of eyes stared at the bill that the waitress left at the edge of the table. He asked her if she was going to pay. She, stunned, said no. And he, just as stunned said "Oh, yes. This meeting was your idea, so this bill is yours". She knew he was cheap—she didn't know he was that cheap. She, now, more eager than ever wanting to get out of his presence, grabbed the bill and took it to the counter. Pastor Bob became somewhat gleeful after that - he took care of her didn't he!! If she is going to ask him out, then, by golly this girl is going to pay.

> Sister remembers her very first boss.
> With words he was never at a loss.
> And, when it came to saying thanks
> Those words rarely came
> And sometimes his language could drive you
> insane.

Sister set out to plan a meeting with him
To talk about what she could do.
She wanted to speak of her work in the parish.
And share with him those tasks
that she really did cherish.

So, away from the rectory and off
to a restaurant they went.
They ate their meal in uncomfortable style,
And after a while,
Their conversation was poor
And she wanted no more
And was ready to leave and go home.

The waitress came over to place the bill on the table
And both expected the other to pay.
Both pairs of eyes were very surprised that
neither party picked up the bill.

He then said to her "I'm not paying, not even a dime.
This meeting was your idea, certainly not mine."
She said this was work and no way would she pay.

But he would not budge—not even a smudge.
And there they were both sitting and wasting their time.

She was stunned at how cheap he could be
And how he could treat her such little dignity.
This was her first job you see, and her
boss said, with a hint of glee;
"If you wanted the meeting, then, by
golly you can pay for the feeding.
I won't be spending a dime."

She picked up the bill and got out of there fast.
And figured that this job just might not last.
Nothing like feeling that you don't matter.
You might as well have your head on a platter.

Disappointed and upset at her first private meeting
with the Pastor, she knew now that there did not seem
to be an avenue of dialogue that would be possible in
this situation. She was under the illusion that she would
learn a lot from her first boss in her first ministry.

A Pondering heart

1. *Was this story just an example of bad manners, miscommunication, or something else?*

2. *How could this have turned out to have a happier ending?*

Sister continued on her way. She continued to serve, pray and teach catechism to children and hold adult education classes for parents. She loved the people and she truly believed that God was found in the people in the pews. When she looked for God, she no longer took it for granted that she would find God in the expected people and places of the church.

When she left to go home that night, she went to pull her car out of the church parking lot. It was then that she discovered

 that all of the hubcaps from her car were missing. She spoke to the maintenance man to ask if he had seen any goings on in the lot that day,

and told him what she discovered. The maintenance man was able to solve the mystery rather quickly. He told her that the associate pastor liked her hubcaps better than his, so he removed hers and put them on his own car!! Wow!

But, of course, the best part is the ending of the story. When the parish planned a farewell party for her they had heard of the hubcap incident–amazed and astonished, they decided, for the farewell party, to decorate the hall with meaningfulness– so, they decorated it… with hubcaps. The point was made– the party was fun–neither pastor nor associate pastor showed up. But, the People of God were present.

A PRETTY RED FORD

Sister received a stipend for the work
that she did in the parish
And the ministry never left her bored.
A car was provided as well for her job.
She had a pretty red Ford

There was a new Pastor in the parish that year
With people's names he was bad
He never remembered their names at all
But he knew the kind of cars that they had.

Mike's car was blue, but his fender was bent.
And his friend down the street had a Ford.
Another one had a Honda for sale,
With a sticker that said "Praise the Lord.'

One time when sister was leaving
work at the end the day
she saw that something was wrong
Because she went to the lot to pick up her car.
And noticed all the hubcaps were gone.

Who would have done that she said to herself.
And she spoke with great dismay
To the maintenance man who was in the lot

And, boy, did he have something to say.

He said: "Well, Father really liked
your hubcaps dear Sister
I saw him remove them one by one.

He then took them and put them on his car
And he had a great deal of fun.

He said: "Sister doesn't need them,
and what does it matter
She has no right to complain.
It's a car that belongs to the parish, not to her
If she thinks it does she's insane.

It's not her car, so what can she say
And praise the good Lord.
Hubcaps or not—
It sure is a pretty red Ford."

Well, what she did say
cannot be repeated,
She felt pretty upset about
the way she was treated.

At the end of the year, she
said farewell to the parish.

> *And they threw a big party for her.*
> *And they helped her get even with the*
> *pastor, perhaps. They decorated the*
> *hall with pretty hubcaps!!! .*

Ministry #2

She remembers her next assignment as a DRE in a parish. The parish staff had complained for years their lack of work space and parish meeting space. There was a plan in place where there would be a complete renovation of the Parish Center so that main parish staff members would have newly renovated and more spacious office space. The Pastor showed her the blueprints that showed her new office that had a spacious room along with a seating area for small group meetings. She was thrilled, until the open house took place. At that time she looked for her office and she saw it on the blueprint, but could not find it in the renovated building, until someone led her down the corridor to a tiny little cubicle that was listed as her new office. She was dumbfounded and approached the pastor for an explanation. He then confessed to her that he had two sets of blueprints made—one was the real blueprint and the second set of blueprints existed solely to 'keep her quiet'. He told her that he did not show her the real blueprint because he could not stand to 'watch her fuss' about the small size of her office. .

A Pondering heart

Where were you when the names were announced?
When the cards were counted,
and the tension mounted?
Where were you when the prizes were given?
When the winners were named
And you felt ashamed
Because
Your name was not even on the list
And you were not even missed.
Now you know that
You really don't count –
And when the day is done and
you had nothing to spare
Know then that you were no one and
'THEY' didn't even care.

A pondering heart

But the more she examined her own conscience the more she realized that the size of her office was not the issue. The issue, of course, was what to do with the continual feeling of being dismissed and disregarded. The other issue was to make sure that she wasn't treating others by dismissing and disregarding them.

Ministry #3

Sister was one of four Sisters living in a convent on the south side of this small town. They loved the little house that the parish had supplied for them. They were there to fulfill a mission—and that mission was to bring Jesus to the men, women, and children… They had a spiritual rhythm to their day. They loved their chapel where they prayed together in the morning and at close of day. They taught religious education to the children and spoke to them of the love of God. They brought communion to the sick in their homes as well as the hospitals. They visited the sick, held hands with the dying, prepared pot-luck dinners for members of committees who worked so hard to also bring Jesus to the lonely and neglected of society. This was their family, this was their home.

Then, a new associate pastor was assigned the parish—newly ordained within the last 5 years. It seemed, rather quickly, that the pastor, feeling tired and depressed, was absent more and more from the parish. This left the new associate to take over the running of the parish and he did this with dictatorial authority and glee.

It did not take him long to meet with the four Sisters in their convent to tell them that the parish had a big financial crisis and could no longer afford to keep up the maintenance of the convent. He was sorry—but he knew that they had another convent on the other side of town. That convent already housed three sisters who worked in another parish school, and there was room for them to move there with little problem. They loved their little house, but they also understood financial crisis and were willing to help the parish during this difficult time.

The move took place, and after months of hard work, the house was left in peace. Was it to be sold so that the parish would have more financial security, or would it just sit there for a while until the finance committee decided its future? After all, the parish needed the money. No one was talking, the pastor seemed oblivious to what was happening, and again, he took off for another vacation.

Within a very short period of time however, the future showed itself in full force. While the pastor was away, while the sisters continued with their ministry, things were in motion in the empty convent. It was completely renovated, and the associate pastor moved out of the rectory and into this house so that he could have his own private residence. It seemed that this was his plan all along.

How did this happen? It seemed to cause some division in the parish—but the pastor never spoke up. The Sisters called a meeting to express their anger, frustration, and feelings of betrayal and yet, nothing changed. The associate pastor was still free to 'run the show.'–And he did. Life went on as it did in many churches, convents, and rectories at that time. Sisters were treated again, as if they did not count.

And, while this was going on, in another part of the state, another group of religious sisters from the same congregation, discovered that they were leaving a parish where they had ministered for 20 years. It's too bad, though, that they had to find out that they were leaving by reading it in the parish bulletin.

Again–the question–***WHERE IS GOD?***

MY SEARCH FOR GOD

I looked for you today
in words that carried
across the miles, and in faces that
carried suspicious smiles.
I did not find you.

I looked for you today
in what I thought were charitable actions,
but instead they led to a lot more factions.
I did not find you.

Instead
I found
A lot of confusion,
And
I was under the illusion
That this is where you were!

Boy! What a surprise!

That instead of you
I found layers of litter and lies

Please—show yourself to me

Be somewhere so I can see.
Unless you've been here all along
And the darkness has been too strong

And I've been surrounded by those same silent cries

Of all those layers of litter and lies.

What was she thinking? That finding God would be easy? That in all the familiar places and people that she came in contact with, that God would be there waiting for her? That her Savior would be right where she thought her Savior would be - waiting for her—ready to show his face, and his heart to her?

It was not that easy… Maybe God was somewhere else.

Ministry #4

She entered into the field of canon law which is the law governing the Catholic Church. She received her canon law degree soon after the 1983 code of canon law allowed women in the degree program. Apparently, before 1983, women weren't smart enough for a canon law degree.

She recalled some of the stories that the older religious sisters in her community would tell her regarding their experience of furthering their education. One sister told her that women were not allowed to take theology courses at one University. However, one professor would leave the classroom door open so that they could sit outside the classroom and listen to the lectures if they wanted to. Another sister remembered that at one particular University women were also not allowed to take theology classes, but women religious were allowed. Why? Because they were not considered 'women'.

Once upon entering into the field of canon law she added to her own story more experiences of no longer wondering what it would feel like to be invisible.

There were 5 women and 25 clergy in the canon law class that she attended. She always felt that she had to prove something–most of the professors would state, when teaching what was considered new material, they would say "but, I don't have to go over this because you learned it already in the seminary."

Unfortunately, the stress did reach an incredible high in her second year of the program when she suffered from inflammation of the optic nerve, caused by incessant grinding of teeth brought about by tension and nerves. The solution was to wear a patch over one eye to help with the double vision. Then, she had to wear a retainer in her mouth because of the incessant grinding of teeth which caused the inflammation of the optic nerve. Then rushing to class one day she fell backwards down a flight of marble steps, and dislocated her shoulder. So–there she was–going to class with a retainer in her mouth, a patch over her eye, and her arm in a sling. Needless to say, she didn't feel invisible then. And, at the end of the two year program, she bought a new pink suit to wear for her oral comprehensives. She wasn't invisible then either.

She remembers her first meeting at a priest's convocation. She found herself sitting at a round table filled with priests and no one spoke to her, or even said hello. No one even introduced themselves or even asked her name. She wanted to scream "H-E-L-L-O, I'M HERE…...But instead, she sat silently- wondering if something was hanging out that shouldn't be. So, she ran to the bathroom to quickly look in the mirror to see if something was hanging from her tooth or coming out of her ear. But, no, she looked okay and that only confused her even more. Again, she felt invisible.

She also remembered her first diocesan Christmas party. The attendance at this party consisted of the direct staff and 30 priests from around the diocese. She was not only new to the diocese, but was one of only three women present at this gathering. She walked to the bar and got herself a strong drink to help calm her nerves. No one spoke to her and she was tempted to just go home. However, she tried to convince herself that she deserved being there–she began talking to herself–also trying to convince herself to get up enough courage to break into any of the closed circles and introduce herself, since no one was inviting her into their circle. She kept saying to herself "I can do this–I can conquer invisibility." Finally, she saw a priest approaching her and she felt relieved. Someone, she thought, is going to talk to me and welcome me into a group. At Last!!! As he approached her, he did not introduce himself to her, but simply took two of his fingers and pressed them on the sleeve of her pin-striped suit. He looked up at her and said "You know, the closer the stripe, the more expensive the suit." Then, he walked away. Then, she walked out of the party.

She also remembered an experience she had five years after receiving her law degree, and after having worked in a canonical position for those past five years. She was sitting having lunch with a priest who was just beginning his canon law degree program and was home during the spring-break. Another priest came over to sit at the table with them, and he said to the priest: "Father, I have a canonical question that I hope you can help me with." And, then he looked over at Sister and said "And, honey, you can listen in if you want".

And guess what? 'Honey' knew the answer to his question, Father did not.

She worked in the canon law office for many years. But, now she was ready for a change and a new phase in her ministry. There were many church positions that she felt qualified for. There were also many positions that she had qualified degrees for, but she still did not qualify for many church positions because she was not a priest, which was the main qualification.

She applied for a new church position, in a new diocese, was interviewed, and was accepted. This was going to be a whole new adventure for her. She was eager, nervous, and excited all at the same time. She was eager to join in work, discussion and camaraderie with the staff who consisted of both clergy and lay, young and old, male and female. There was an incredible amount of work and she began to take on the tasks with enthusiasm and seriousness.

Well, it did not take long for her to describe the atmosphere of the office - stark and impersonal. She really thought that because of her long history and vast experience in church ministry that her opinion and many years of experience would be valued and welcomed. She soon discovered that the opposite was more the case. She was considered the stranger, the odd one out. Her opinion was not sought after and, if she offered her opinion it was not welcomed.

And, rules were set in place. Words were not to be exchanged because you were told that you were 'too busy to talk.' Even though she had years of experience it did not take long to feel like a nobody.

Even eating lunch seemed like a problem. The rest of the staff were told that they could not eat their lunch at their desk, because the desk was 'your work space.' And, the only other space was the conference room and that room could only be used for 'conferences'. The only place left was your car which was parked in the lot under the searing heat. Your heated car became your lunch room.

Gifts were considered bribes and could not be accepted. She remembers a client whom she helped. This client who was so grateful to her for her assistance that she sent her a beautiful box of candy and assorted cookies. Unfortunately she was not able to accept this gift, since, she was told, accepting it would send the wrong message because it could be interpreted as 'accepting a bribe.'

Making private calls on your cell phone were not allowed, and using the office phone for private calls was also not allowed. She was told that the staff has set the standard:

"you never see anyone using their cell phone for personal phone calls, so take note, you are not to use it either." What this supervisor did not realize is that other staff members did use their cell phone–but hid in the bathroom when they needed to make a personal call.

There was a national conference that took place in the diocese that year. The staff were all involved in the planning, operations, conferences, and introduction of speakers. The bosses in her office all had a major role in introducing speakers, or even being a speaker at one of the events. She waited to see what her task would be–only to find out that her major role was to pass out the program for the opening prayer–and then to pass out the lunch menu.

THE RULES OF THE GAME

My name is rule and order, and rigid.
Some days I'm hot and some days I'm frigid.
I can tell you that talk is not good for you
Unless it's me you're talking to.

Discuss your problem? Oh, no they say.
You just simply bow and obey.
And talk doesn't help unless it's with me.

And God forbid if you're not able to see

That the rule comes first and people are naught.
If you don't follow this, then you'll get caught.
And lose your job that you thought you had.
And that's what's sad
That you've been had.

Because all along you thought they knew
And trusted you.
And that fell through
The jokes on you.

So, just do your work—cut your losses
Don't look for trouble, just obey your bosses
Just keep to yourself and bide your time.
But, it's the rules serving no one, that's the real crime.

So she continued going to work every day- making the best attempt at minding her own business. But she knew she could not cope with the continued feeling and experience of being invisible, and often even discarded. She hesitated to take any initiative on her own for fear of breaking a policy or facing scrutiny or suspicion. Where were all of the spiritual and corporal works of mercy that she learned at home and in her catholic upbringing?

What is all of this supposed to mean? She remembers being told not to forget that the most important law of the church was the last one that is noted in the code of canon law—Canon 1752 states: "…..with due regard for canonical equity and having before one's eyes the salvation of souls, which is always the supreme law of the church." What happened with that?

Have you ever felt betrayed?
Abandoned or abused?
Have you ever looked at someone's face?
And felt only more confused?

Have you ever felt dismissed
In thought and word and deed
And only realized much too late
That you were just deceived?

You gave your life to God
And you firmly held belief
That these leaders of the church
Would bring you some relief.

Relief in knowing the way to God
Is sacrifice and prayer
Instead they showed you something else
That you found hard to bear

> ***Deceived by those who ran the church***
> ***And you were just its slave***
> ***And cast aside, without a thought***
> ***Again you were betrayed***

- Please don't tell her that this has all been in vain! She often tried to remind herself of her patron saint, St. Joan of Arc. St. Joan was burned at the stake one year, and declared a saint the next. That was quite a turn-around- a little too much drama for her, but a happy ending none-the-less. Could her ending be happy as well?

Or, should she just do her work and shrug the cynicism and the meanness and keep searching for the divine—again is the divine found within the search?

A pondering heart

Can you name an experience or experiences where you felt 'invisible'? How did you react or respond to that experience?

Is there any line in particular, in the above poem that you can relate to? Have you ever felt betrayed, abandoned, abused, dismissed, or deceived? If so, how did you respond?

- What is in her heart? Is it fear, sadness, wonder?

Ministry #5

However, in the end, perhaps her qualifications, her education, and her experience were recognized. Sister was appointed a new position in the diocese. She received no word of support, or encouragement from her previous bosses. Instead she was told by one of them that it will take less than a year for the bishop to realize what a mistake he made in appointing her. This same boss believed that only clerics could serve in the position that she was offered, and therefore, he told her that anything she would do in this position would be declared 'invalid' and it would only create more work for him.

And so, there she sat—in her new office, in a brand new office building where all of the diocesan offices were now located. Some of her tasks consisted of more canonical responsibilities, and In addition, she was also in a position to offer advice to Pastors and parish directors regarding sacramental questions, and any other canonical questions that may arise. Hopefully, this position will bring her respect and assure her of more confidence as a competent woman in the church. She needed respect from others so that respect for herself could grow, since her earlier treatment by clergy staff only lowered her level of self-confidence and raised her level of insecurity.

She found herself surrounded by people who were competent, helpful, and caring. She settled into her office and said to herself: "Everything will be all right. Each day will feel better than the day before."

However, as the years went by–her confidence seemed to go by as well.

There were many painful moments–when the church doors seem to close on people who really needed help. The doors were closed and no one was there to listen to people's stories of grief, or their loneliness, or their questions. Was she one of those who didn't take the time to listen? There were, of course, true pastors who spread the gospel with their lives. They lived, laughed, and loved the people they served. They served with heroism and humility. They never took credit for the good that they had done, but gave God and the People of God the credit.

But, other so-called leaders, became too concerned with being master of their flock, not pastor of their flock. And if one attempted to step in and make a change one became bombarded with the phrase 'this is none of your business.'

One day, without a knock on the door, a priest who recently was named a Monsignor, strode into her office without welcome or introduction. He knew her name however, and said it sharply and with authority–and then said these words: "I just came from the bathroom and I need to report to you that the plumbing is not working and I left my 'belongings' in toilet number two. Take care of it." Then he marched out of her office. She sat in her seat for a while, not saying a word to him or to anyone since she was kind of frozen in thought and……….. Why me? She thought–why is he telling me? Then, - it dawned on her–maybe this explains, at last, what was missing in her job description, yet something that she spent a great

deal of time doing–and this 'Monsignor' made it all clear to her now–and that is that she spends a great deal of time cleaning up the 'belongings' that so many of the clergy leave behind for someone else to clean up. The 'belongings' left behind is what is making a mess of this church.

Yes, in many ways clericalism is alive and well and active. She was reminded of canon 517.2 which allows lay leadership of parishes. One problem with that canon however, is that it states that lay leadership of parishes is allowed if there is a 'lack of priests.' It does not say "a lack of qualified priests." And some of these "not-so-qualified' are the ones who leave their 'belongings' behind - the layers of litter and lies that need to be recognized for what they are—someone has to clean it all up, and then, it needs to be put away for good. Oftentimes, this does become her real job.

And again, she asks herself........Where is God in all of this mess?

PUT IT ALL AWAY

When you played games with toys and stuff
And things got rough,
Did you ever hear your Momma say
Enough,
Put it all away my child, put it all away?

The toys were gathered up real soon
In paper bags, and, with a broom
Were cleared and stuffed into a room.
Enough, you said.
You put it all away, my child, you put it all away.
You followed your Momma's rule.
Which was not cruel,
It was a tool
To help arrange each day, hard and fought.
With no more clutter and no more thought,

You did what you were taught,
You said "enough..- You put it all away,
my child, you put it all away.

At that time it was easy.
You knew what to do.
You followed the rule
And the rule helped you.

But today, how to do that now
How to put it all away—the
fear, the grief, with no relief
And no one there to say, with love
Enough, put it all away, my
child, just put it all away?

But how do you stuff pain and confusion
into a drawer, and say no more?
How do you say "enough... I've had enough?

It can't be stuffed into a drawer
You have to speak and say "no more'
Because each day, there is another scheme.
And then, you scream
And say ENOUGH
And now, tell them straight
WITHOUT DELAY

DAM IT... PUT IT ALL AWAY.

**Because your games of torture and your lies, are now
No longer a surprise.
I've figured you out...
And, without a doubt.
There's now no way out.
You can no longer bluff.
I've had enough, ENOUGH, I SAY.
Now YOU, PUT IT ALL AWAY.**

Why am I here, she asked herself again? Is that my real job? Where is God in all of this mess, in all of this dysfunction? What to do? How to go on? How to clean all of this up and put it away so that the real meaning of life and love and faith can survive.

Where are you O God?

She continued the search. And, she began to grow in wisdom as well. Her prayer and her faith in God led her to the real understanding that the church is not the perfect society but the People of God. She began to realize that of course, if she can't find God it doesn't matter. Because God has already found her.

God took her hand and told her to look beyond the presumed places of God's presence and look instead in the unexpected, in the wounded and often the discarded. God spoke to her and said "Here I am." She sought the face of God and God led her to the treasure hidden in the field. She sought the treasure and found the face of God in the faces of the faithful.

Chapter Four

THE FACES OF THE FAITHFUL

A. *The Face of a friend*

Her eyes stopped to gaze at a picture of her friend Sarah who passed away several years ago. She began to recall her last visit with her when she was still alert and able to communicate. On that day she found Sarah in her room simply gazing intently, quietly, and peacefully, out her window, watching the children next door playing outside in their yard. The sky was adorned with shapely clouds and the leaves of the tall trees in the yard swayed as if dancing to the wind. And under that tree sat two little girls playing near a small pool of water–laughing and swirling little tree twigs in the water, creating little characters out of the twigs and turning them into a playful backyard of little movie characters. Sarah could not take her eyes off of them–their sweet creativity and their joy in the little magic of the moment. Sarah then looked up at her friend and smiled and said "God is in our midst." She thought perhaps that Sarah had had a vision because those words seemed to come from nowhere–when she suddenly realized where they did come from. Those words were Sarah's words–the children gave her a glimpse of God, and, for her, what she saw in Sarah's face was the face of God.

How many times, she asked, have I missed the face of God because I was too busy looking somewhere else? She remembered the following story:

"There was a Sufi called Mullah Nasrudin who smuggled treasure across the border and masterfully eluded the guards. Every day for four years he would parade back and forth, and with every crossing the guards knew he was hiding expensive goods that he would sell for outrageous amounts of money on the other side. But despite their thorough searches, and despite the fact that they could see that he was prospering, they could find nothing in the saddle of the donkey he rode. Finally, years later, after

Mullah Nasrudin had moved to another country, the frontier guard said, "Okay, you can tell me now. What were you smuggling?" The mullah smiled broadly and said, "My dear friend, I was smuggling donkeys."

A Pondering heart

Can you name a time, or an experience you have had where you realized later that you missed the face of God because you were too busy looking someplace else and; only realized later that the face of God was right in front of you?

She thought - there may be times when we are tempted to determine where and when we will meet God. There is an old Jewish epigram that says, "God is not a kindly old uncle, he is an earthquake." Are there times when you restrict your search for 'kindly old uncles' and overlook the earthquake?

Do we sometimes have to leave behind our certainty that we already know where God is?

Yes, God is in our midst. And often, God is found in unexpected places —even in an encounter that at first appears odd or even puzzling. And, if at first we can't find God in our search, then pray that God will send us a message. Sarah certainly sent a message. And, Sarah did not have to look far to find God. Sarah saw the face of God in the children in their simple playfulness, and Sarah's friend saw the face of God when gazing at the face of Sarah. When we see the face of God in another human being—then, we offer them our own face. If it is filled with kindness, care, love and generosity, then those people we meet will be encountering God through us. Isn't that our task? To show others the face of God? Not a face of anger, or bitterness, or conflict, but the face of God?

B. The Face of Erwin

She left her place of employment, and did not know what would be next. She gave herself a rest and relied on the spirit of Christmas to find the divine.

It was Christmas Eve, and her friends asked her to join them as they drove to the soup kitchen to help serve a Christmas dinner to those in need.

This is where she met Erwin. She was haunted by Erwin after that Christmas day. He didn't mean to haunt her. It wasn't his intention. He didn't wake up in the morning and have that marked on his calendar to do for that day. She also didn't wake up that morning with 'haunting' on her mind.

But, there he was.–The eyes were large and haunting–revealing the fact that there were many hidden stories to tell.

"Where do you live"? Sister asked.

What a silly question to ask of one who has no home.

"What happened"? Was her next question.

And then she watched his face transform to such unutterable grief–a slow, tearing, and twisting and torture that she put him through by having to answer her questions–for having to say the words that choked him and choked her...

I have no home. I have no bed... my family all dead... And no one but me. I lost my family, my home, my job, my will to live. And now I have this sack with my home inside.

At one time I owned my own company–but not anymore–I own nothing but this sack. My home is a stoop, a step, a spot. I read a book a day. I read all of Cathleen Coulter, Pat Conroy, and John Grisham.

I have a love of cookouts too. My favorite is deviled eggs–you need to try two types of mustard to get the right flavor, and, whatever you do, don't let the eggs boil too long in the water.

I love that you ask me questions–you seem to care about me. Will you be my friend? Will you come back and visit me? When you come back we can speak about books and eggs.

But, don't ask me what happened. I am liable to cry and never stop. They may not let me back in the library to rest my head.

Someone bought me a backpack so I can carry my home and books with me.

So–on this Christmas day, off he went–out in the cold, hoping for a warmer day tomorrow, and, maybe, a new book.

And, she wonders where God is???–God is in the heart of one who mourns.

She went in search for the divine that day–and God introduced her to Erwin.

<u>*A Pondering heart*</u>

Where did this seeker find God on this Christmas Eve?

In our search for God, are we often surprised to find God in unexpected places?

<u>*C. The Face of Jeremie and Benoit*</u>

RWANDA

The country of a thousand hills - ah, the hills, the waves of green everywhere you looked.

Roads, untamed
Heat, choking, and energy, vanishing.
Tremble of earth and hill, of heart and soul, torched and troubled.

And the birds still sing.
And everyone walks everywhere
Lame ones, weak ones, little ones,
Strong ones, with their wood and rice, and wheat, and
Coffee beans and banana leaves, and water.
Walking...everywhere... in light... no light. In darkness, no problem.

Babies hidden under mother and

The endless chant

OF

JAMAIS ENCORE!!
NEVER AGAIN!!

In this country of a thousand hills, and the people say
A thousand problems—where the labor is ENDLESS
One carries water, and other people's lives.

And the birds still sing.

And vegetation still rises from the earth, along with
Hope and forgiveness.

And the flowers still bloom
And the children still play
And the mother still gives birth
And the plants still grow, and the people still infirm,
And life still goes on—in shacks, in huts, and sheds
And,
Forests, and in one's soul.

And, for me, there lies the mystery.

How, why... do the birds still sing?

Rwanda is a country located in Central Africa and is one of the smallest countries on the African mainland. Its geography is dominated by mountains in the west and savannas to the east, with numerous lakes throughout the country. Rwanda–called a country of a thousand hills–the beauty of this country is beyond belief. The Rwandan people are drawn from one cultural and linguistic group, the Banyarwanda, yet, within this group there are three subgroups: the Hutu, the Tutsi, and the Twa.

In just 100 days in 1994, about 800,000 people were slaughtered in Rwanda by ethnic Hutu extremists. They were targeting members of the minority Tutsi community, as well as their political opponents, irrespective of their ethnic origin. The world did not step in to stop the slaughter.

The Rwandan Patriotic Front, a trained military group consisting of Tutsis who had been exiled in earlier years, entered Rwanda and slowly took over the country. When they had full control, the genocide was finally stopped.

In 2009, she, along with another sister, entered the country of Rwanda to help teach English to her religious  community of Sisters, since the government was in the process of changing its national language from French to English. The change seemed to take over the country overnight, with all of the street signs, along with everything else, suddenly transformed from the words in French to the words in English. There she was, in the hills of this beautiful country, staying with Rwandan Sisters who worked with the orphans. And, there was the unique experience of meeting God again, in an unexpected place.

Because, there in the hills, she met Jeremie and Benoit—two brothers whose family did not survive the slaughter of one million Tutsis in 100 days of killings.

And there they were! How could this happen—how could machetes take over a country of such beauty—and, if ever there was a soul searching for God it was then.

And yet—there was Jeremie and Benoit—as she trudged up the hill thinking, can I make it? Can I make the dusty trail part of my home—can I stand once again near the site where skeletons hung on display so that no one would ever forget the horrors that ravaged this beautiful country. Can she cope? Can she hope...as well, that peace would come upon this land?

Then, a moment of transformation–because, as she trudged up the hill, suddenly she saw Jeremie and Benoit– with arms outstretched running and running toward her as if running into the arms of their mother–their mother who was chopped and discarded and thrown into Lake Kivu. They ran and she ran as well. She ran toward them and offered them a moment of warmth and mothering - they wrapped themselves around her, and she did the same to them. And, for a moment, she took their pain away. And she knew with such certainty that God was there– they helped to take her doubt away.

Yes, God is in our midst. And often, God is found in unexpected places –even in an encounter that at first appears odd or even puzzling. And, if at first we can't find God in our search, then pray that God will send us a message. And God will reveal to us the face of the divine in our neighbor. When we see the face of God in another human being–then, we offer them our own face. If it is filled with **kindness, care, love and generosity, then those** people we meet will be encountering God through us. Isn't that our task - to show others the face of God? Not a face of anger, or bitterness, or conflict, but the face of God?

THE SEARCH FOR THE DIVINE

Faceless and frantic, running and weaving
In and out of people's lives...as well as one's own.

Dropped paper, garbage in the streets, as well
as an empty shell that once held a life.

Searching for softness, and generosity,
a smile, or even just
A nod of notice
A gift of gratitude
A thank- you
A door being opened
A child held in love
A sadness transformed into joy
A window of giving - a truth exposed.

A life turning toward wholeness once again.

One window
One touch
One step
One glance

Won over,
By one small gesture.

That's not asking for too much is it?
One small glimmer of hope
That the world has not given up on the divine?

D. Where is God in the face of Grief?

When does God show up? Or, is God always there and the 'showing up' part depends on us? What about "O God, my God, why have you abandoned me"? When this seeker suffered the death of her sister, in the darkest night of her soul, when life seemed shattered and dark, when there seemed to be no reason to live—it was then that she looked for God—searched for God—banged on every door and floor and powers that be. But, to her, because of her pain and feeling of abandonment God was gone. God didn't just disappear, but God was no longer God. There was no God. There was just sweat and tears and wracking nerves and feelings of total and absolute abandonment. Every night, every day, the begging would come out of her mouth and heart. Please God, show yourself to me she begged,—send me a sign that all will be well and this isn't the end, and heaven will unite us some day. This wracking pain went on day after day after day. She needed a sign Oh God—send her a sign.

Then, she said: "I've had enough–this is it–either a sign or I am completely lost. I've spent my life telling people to trust you–and here I am, unable to place my faith in you. Please help me again–help me not to give up on you.

She then sat down with the Bible in her hand - the Word of God.:

Send me a word from you O God, she implored, so that I can believe that I will once again meet my soul-mate and all will be well. She spoke plainly to God: "God, I am going to open this Bible and I am going to open to a page and I'm going to place my finger on a passage in this Bible–and that passage better be a message directly from you to me. When I read that passage may I never again doubt that you are my God and you have not abandoned me. This is it God. This is your last chance–but not only yours, but mine as well."

She then knelt on the floor of that dark, quiet room–she placed the Bible in front of her and then she closed her eyes–and opened the Bible and placed her finger on a page and a passage in front of her. She then opened her eyes ready to receive a message from God. She then read the line that her right index finger had rested on, and this is what she read:

Song of Solomon 8:6 "love is stronger than death."

"Could this possibly be what you are saying to me"–she asked her God?–*"That there really is no doubt that this will all work out? That love will win out in the end - that death does not have the last word?"*

She did not know how to work this out. She needed to believe that this was truly a message from the God who she was searching for –and that this God is a God of love, a God of eternal love–and love will win out in the end. It is stronger than her fear and grief, and rests in her heart, and, it is stronger than death itself. God has revealed God's self in the face of a grieving heart.

So - she spoke these words to her sister:

"Can you come and visit me–so I can hear how you sound, and see how you look, and how you laugh, and what you would think about all of this now?

What was the purpose of your early departure?

Can you come and visit me–and ask me how I've been– ask me how I survived all these years without you? Because I was so convinced that I would never be happy again–Can you ask me about relationships and how they changed over the course of years—how I saw my own image enlightened, matured?

Ask me how I am - Where I fit in this universe—about my struggles and loves and journeys. Join me on this porch—with my flowers, and birds, and silence, and happiness, which I thought I would never have again, and ask me how I am—and how I did it?

And then, tell me what will happen now—and what the future will hold.

Or,

Just come and visit me on this porch and we can enjoy the flowers and birds together—and, we can reminisce once again—like old times...

And, maybe we can, at least, begin to understand why it all happened the way it did— or, maybe you can just come and visit me on this porch."

THE GARDEN

Will we ever walk together?
Holding hands so strong and firm

Looking at the colors glitter
In the garden that we yearn?

They are full of many colors
Purple, red and yellow true
And the leaves are stretching
toward us
In the calm and gentle dew.
Will we ever walk together?
Down the path of heaven bright
Looking at the flowers and petals
At the saviors eternal light

Oh, if I could only wonder
What that time could truly be
When you and I will be together
What joy! What ecstasy!

Will we ever walk together?
In the rows of tulips bright
Filled with ever-lasting colors
O My Jesus what a sight.

Tell me God who art in heaven
That this time will truly be
When you and I will be together
Oh what joy, what ecstasy.

Where is God in the grief?
She finds herself still searching for relief.

Chapter Five

THE VOICE OF
THE DIVINE

She continued her journey—her journey of faith in her search for God. She began to look beyond the presumed places of God's presence and found God in the unexpected, in the wounded and the often discarded. She sought the face of God and her discovery led her to the treasure hidden in the field. She sought the treasure and found the face.

Again—she began to relive some of the memories of her search—and then, she heard a voice—a voice that called her name and again, she wondered if she would have discovered this God sooner had she paid attention to the call–the call–the voice that spoke to her through the voices of the voiceless. Here–this led her to another search–not only for the face of God–but the voice of God as well–the voice that often spoke to her, but was unheard or ignored.

She, again, turned to Jesus because he can teach us how to 'hear' the voice of God. What did Jesus do? He first sought the place of silence so that he could listen to the silence within. Continually Jesus withdrew from people, daily life activities, and the demands of his ministry to be alone with His God and listen.

The priority of Jesus' solitude and silence is everywhere in the Gospels. It is how he began his ministry, and how he made important decisions. It is how he dealt with troubling emotions like grief. It is how he dealt with the constant demands of his ministry and cared for his soul. It is how he taught his disciples. It is how he prepared for important ministry events. It is how he prepared for his death.

Jesus went to the desert–to hear the voice of God. Of course, it is not always possible to go to a desert but maybe there is a way to flee from the noise without and within so that we can hear the Lord calling us.

Scripture tells us that God calls us by name—God calls and beckons us to listen to the still, sacred voice of the one who loves us 'beyond our thoughts beyond our fears, from death unto life.'

God speaks to us in the silence of our heart, and our response can be: "Speak Lord, your servant is listening." But, she questioned whether the voice of God can be drowned out by the noises inside our head.

Is there a difference between sound and noise? Noise is everywhere. Noise can be described as an unwanted sound, especially one that is disturbing and disruptive, and studies have shown that noise can actually increase stress and cause all sorts of health problems. Sounds, on the other hand, can be comforting and can bring to mind feelings of safety, comfort, or joy. It could be a piece of music, a person's voice, or it could be a sound that brings to mind a memory long forgotten. Is the world today so full of noise that we can't hear or distinguish the sound of God's voice? How difficult is it to hear the sound of God's voice if we are bombarded by noise from all directions?

Hearing the voice of God amidst the noises of the world

As she pondered the mystery of hearing and recognizing the voice of God she began to recall the sounds and the noises from her childhood. She knew the difference then. She recalled the sounds that were familiar and comforting. She recalled sitting near the railroad tracks, waiting for her grandfather to return home. He was the conductor of the train, and there she sat, with her sister—amidst the weeds and thistles brushing against their backs- they spoke not a word—because they did not want to miss the distant sound of the whistle of the train. And, when they heard that familiar and long awaited for sound they knew that 'grandpa' would soon be home. That train whistle was definitely a sound—not a noise.

Another sound from the past was the old ice cream truck bringing popsicles and ice cream to the projects where she lived. She was not old enough yet for school, but she was old enough to follow that big old truck as it trudged up the mighty hill. She and her sister were there to follow it around the project. They waited to hear the toot, toot, toot, of the horn from that old truck—knowing that they would soon be comforted with vanilla, chocolate, strawberry, buttercream or peach ice cream. That toot, toot, toot, was definitely not noise, but an incredible and heartwarming sound.

Once she began to attend school she remembers the sound that the chalk made on the blackboard when Sister Mary Louise would spell out the corporal and spiritual works of mercy. The class would memorize the list of virtues and be prepared to defend the faith with courage and confidence, even though they were only eight years old. She also remembers the sound of Sister Mary Louise's clicker telling the class when to stand (click), genuflect (click), sit or kneel (click, click). This sound of the clicker was not exactly like the sound of the ice cream truck or the sound of the train. But, it was the sound of discipline and innocent fervor forever etched in a catholic school child's memory.

Upon entering adulthood new sounds have remained fresh in her memory–like the sound of laughter when a good joke was told, or the sound of weeping when someone's death was near–the sound of home and the sound of the familiar–the sound that made one bathe in its comfort and halt in its pain. The sound that made one stop–the sounds that today bring back the memories of what was once worth listening to.

But, today, there are sirens and horns, the beeping of store scanners, the vehicle backing up, the roar of an engine, the hand blower in the restrooms, the digital ding of an e-mail message, the chatter and bellow of words coming out of voices that yearn to be heard or helped or healed. There is the constant noise that muffles the voices of the voiceless –and there is the sound within our own soul calling for inner peace and comfort which remain unheard because of the chatter going on in and around us.

Yes - God calls us to enter into the silence of our own heart—to flee the noise within and without so that we can hear what the Lord God has to say.

Yet—there are times when she found herself afraid—afraid of the silence, and afraid of being alone. She was afraid of what she would hear—not God's voice—but her own voice or the voices of others going on in her head.

You are not good enough, the voices say, or you don't deserve that job, that promotion, that friendship. Or, perhaps that voice is surfacing a memory that has long been hidden, but never completely forgotten, and, in the silence, it comes to haunt you.

Once, when she went back to visit her home town, she went to rest on a park bench in the neighborhood where she grew up. She closed her eyes and tried to steady her breathing, but all she could feel was inner panic and anxiety. A flood of memories haunted her attempt at solitude. When she closed her eyes all she could see were the childhood years of playing hopscotch with her sister, the times they ran through that park to get to the merry-go-round, and ended the day at Ed's grocery store for his famous fudgesicles. Those were happy memories, but she grieves them as well, because her sister is gone, died too young, and is not here to reminisce with her. Instead of arriving at inner peace, she found myself regretting any attempt at solitude.

She knows that God speaks to her in the silence–but, she is often afraid of the silence, for fear of what the other inner voice that wells within her will say. So–she keeps busy. It's not that she doesn't want to hear the voice of God. She would welcome it with joy. But, she was afraid of what else she would hear if she allowed herself to enter into the silence. Will she only hear her own voice, expressing regret, or guilt, or fear, or more grief? She yearns for solitude–but is afraid of it at the same time. As a child, she was never alone–even in her mother's womb she was not alone. Now–when she is alone–she doesn't want to be afraid of fleeing from the silence.

So–she began to ask herself some serious questions. Have I given up or given in too quickly, she asked? In my search for God, am I the one who is not really listening?

When she was a child and she tried to learn how to play the piano, or tried to learn a new language, did she give up on that too soon as well? Or, did she in the end, listen attentively to her teachers who never gave up on her and told her just to keep studying, to keep practicing and 'with practice it will come."? She listened to her teachers and they had confidence in her. Is there a lesson here for her?

Jesus says: "I am with you." How many times do we find these words spoken to us in the Scriptures, "I am with you?" And, Jesus also says: "Come to me, all you who labor and are heavily burdened and I will give you rest. "For my yoke is easy and my burden light." She then began to understand that one doesn't go to the silence alone. Instead, one goes to the silence to find God, and God is there waiting in the silence for her to come. God is our teacher, God has confidence in us and will not allow us to fail. We need to keep practicing, and, as our teachers have said…" and it will come." The best way to learn to be silent is to practice. One student of contemplative prayer was heard to say that the best way to learn how to practice contemplative prayer was to just 'sit down and be quiet.'

She knows now that she cannot give up, and God does not give up calling each of us by name, and she knows now that she must not give up in her longing to enter into the inner desert of her soul. Because what we find there may surprise us and it may change our lives. We are not alone in our desire to hear the voice of God. Many spiritual leaders faced the same challenges that we face in our spiritual journey–how to block out the noise in order to hear the sound of God's voice. These spiritual leaders can help us in our journey to hear the voice of God and distinguish it from the other sounds that bombard us from all directions.

Thomas Merton, a Trappist monk, who wrote extensively about the contemplative life, states that God speaks to us in the silence. He writes: "Our being is silence, but our existence is noisy. Our actions, tend to be noisy but when they stop, there is a ground of silence which is always there." (Springs of contemplation, p 61). He continues by stating that silence ultimately denotes presence, not just the absence of sound.

So–how can we stop the noise around us so that we can hear the voice of God speaking to us in the silence? We must first learn to make friends with the silence, then it no longer becomes the enemy. If we can find our center, there we will find God waiting. We need to learn not to fight the distractions and the inner voices, but befriend them and then let them go, one by one, let them go, and then, let God do the rest. Then we will be open to hearing the sound of God's voice. And, the voice will be clear in its words and in its message–for the voice is saying' you are my beloved, my delight."

And so, the search for God continues –
And the journey leads to many surprises
God may not be where we have always looked
God may not be in the structure, and the rules
Instead..
God is discovered in the faces of the poor, the suffering,
In the unexpected people and places
And
We may not hear God's voice when hearing the commands,
and the do's and don'ts of being a 'registered church member'
Instead, God is discovered in the voices

Of the vulnerable and the voiceless.
And perhaps the voice of God can be found in the heart of
one who listens
With openness and grace.

The Voice of Calvin

There she was—sitting peacefully on a bus. It had been quite a while since she was a passenger on a greyhound bus, traveling a six hour ride to the other end of the state. It was quite crowded, but she had a seat to herself and consciously prepared herself for a quiet, peaceful, ride—maybe even catching an afternoon nap after an exhausting weekend.

One of the many stops on this bus route was a stop at a Veterans hospital. This is where the passengers on this bus met Calvin. Calvin boarded the bus, spoke and greeted everyone down the aisle as he trudged to a seat right behind her. She had hoped, against hope, that Calvin also had the desire for an afternoon nap. But that, she guessed, was asking too much. Instead, Calvin was more interested in conversation than quiet.

Soon, Calvin began a conversation with the woman sitting to his right. The conversation however was more like a built in microphone system that carried Calvin's voice throughout the bus. "Are you Catholic?" he asked the woman who was seated next to him. She responded with the words "Yes, I am." He then asked her: "Do you pray to the Blessed Mother"? With a little more exasperation in her voice, she responded "Yes." Calvin then said to her: "Good, would you like to pray the rosary with me?" Her answer, she thought, would put an end to the conversation when she responded "No, I pray my beads privately."

Instead of bringing this whole public conversation to rest, Calvin began to pray the rosary out loud, every decade of the Rosary, every Hail Mary, Glory Be, and Our Father... on and on and on... from joyful, glorious and sorrowful mysteries. Calvin's voice filled this greyhound vehicle with his prayers, and the prayers that seemed to echo from his heart.

At first, she was annoyed, very annoyed. Who needed an annoyance such as Calvin for a six hour bus ride? He was a veteran, with a limp, and a loud voice that carried from front row to back row. She labeled him as a nuisance and was quite content when he finally arrived at his destination and said goodbye to each one as he exited the bus.

This nuisance was gone at last. At first, she breathed a sigh of relief. Then, she did not know if one would call it a moment of insight or a sudden revelation–something struck her like a bolt of lightning. She wondered if she had just missed the voice of God by dismissing the voice of a nuisance. Bang–it was right in front of her and she dismissed it. She suddenly remembered the fairy tale of the Princess and the Frog. By dismissing the frog, the nuisance, she lost her chance of meeting the charming prince. She missed the kingdom because she failed to recognize the king.

The voice of Calvin was the voice of a nuisance–that was her label for him. And, maybe this voice was the voice of God, speaking to her, and saying "This is who you are called to be–the nuisance in society". A nuisance is one who is in the wrong place at the wrong time. A nuisance is one who is in the way. A nuisance is one who nags and nags and nags about something until you give in or give up. A nuisance is one who hears the beat of a different drummer—one who is out of step with the crowd.

A public nuisance is not one who sits back meekly and ignorantly but is one who pursues boldly and dramatically the kingdom of God. A public nuisance is someone who reverses society's order of things, someone who pricks society's conscience and forces society to take one step beyond its own logic.

The voice of Jesus rings true now—the voice of God may be found in the voices of those considered a nuisance. That much Calvin taught her and can teach us as well—we need to listen to the Calvin's in our lives—certainly the face of God may be right in front of us—but, the voice of God may be ringing in our ears and we paid no heed.

With all of this in mind we are all called to follow the footsteps of Jesus who was the greatest nuisance of all. So much so that he was put to death—and that he witnessed for all of us what it truly means to be Christian and what it truly means to be a public witness in the church, and in our world.

<u>A pondering heart</u>

What does it actually mean to be a 'nuisance for the kingdom of God?'

Is God's voice calling us to be that nuisance?

With all of this in mind we are all called to follow the footsteps of Jesus who was the greatest nuisance of all. So much so that he was put to death—and that he witnessed for all of us what it truly means to be Christian and what it truly means to be a public witness in the church, and in our world.

Chapter Six

CONCLUSION

She pondered all of this—pondered her search for the Divine. Had she been looking in the wrong places and silently muting the voice of God?

Then she heard a voice that said
YES -
Amidst the thunder, the noise, the treason and intimidation—she heard the voice of God. God said:

- See the mothers holding their babies with love and affection.

- See the crippled and lame being taken care of by a loved one who held them steady as they entered the church doors or stood in line for confession.

- See the face of the homeless man who lost his entire family in a car accident–he asked you for help in getting a library card because he was trying to find a book that would comfort him. You gave him the Bible… and he wept.

This is the real church–not the 'perfect society' the pre-Vatican words that some choose to use to describe church -but the real church–the People of God–those ignored, invisible, or considered a nuisance. God said "My presence is so perfectly made visible, not in ecclesiastical structure, but in the people you serve. Look at my Son–there you will find me–my message, my teaching, and the real church."

So, that's what she decided to do–She went to the Scriptures. She discovered that Jesus broke the mold. Jesus broke the rules. He didn't disregard the rules, but he tells the people; "I have come not to abolish the law but to fulfill it." (Matt: 5:17). Jesus surprised those who thought they had the road to salvation all figured out. Then, Jesus surprised them by turning it all upside down. The first are really last–and the last will be the first. The poor might be the ones with all of the riches—and the rich ones may be filled with poverty.

And, if women did not think they had a place in the church because they were treated as unworthy, lower class, and certainly not as smart as men—then, Jesus shows them just the opposite.

Jesus continually shows that women matter. And a church that cannot answer a resounding "yes, women do matter' is no church of Jesus Christ.

Look at the example Jesus gives us with regard to the treatment of women:

1. Jesus speaks with a Samaritan woman as she draws water from a well, and he even asks her for a drink. Men at that time, were not to speak to women in public, and this act really stunned Jesus' disciples. It was a scandal, but Jesus spoke to her anyway. In fact Jesus' conversation with this woman is the longest conversation recorded between Jesus and any person in the gospels, and it is with a woman, and a non-Jew.

2. Jesus also allows a woman who was declared a sinner, to anoint his feet. This move on his part

broke all of the cleanliness law for the Jews. But, again, not only does Jesus not stop the woman, but he draws attention to her faithfulness and he tells Simon: "Wherever this good news is proclaimed in the whole world, what she has done will be told in remembrance of her." (Matthew 26: 13).

3. And Jesus breaks another 'rule.' In Luke 10: 42, Jesus affirms Mary's decision to forgo the typical female hostess role and sit at Jesus' feet, a place normally reserved for male disciples. And then, he says "Mary has chosen the better part." Here is Jesus again, breaking another norm.

4. And, the church spends a great deal of time preaching about Jesus' resurrection and his appearance to the disciples. Yet, what is often missing in the telling, is that Jesus first appeared to Mary Magdalene. And, what does he tell her? He says: "Go. Tell the good news of my resurrection. Let my disciples know I am very much alive."

This is where God is–God is in those we serve. Jesus shows us perfectly where God is found.

It was all becoming clearer to her as she trudged this journey of discovery–that God is where love and service is –God is alive and well, and perfectly visible in the words, actions, gestures of love towards one another. This is the true church –and where the true church is revealed– the face of God is revealed as alive and well.

Again, if we turn to Jesus, he tells us that we reveal the face of God when we care for one another, in love, in generosity, in selflessness and self-giving. Jesus wanted people to know that if they see the face of God in loving and caring for their neighbor, then they will discover that the sacred is in their midst. Jesus tells us that where there is love, there is God. God is here–in our loving, in our caring, in our generosity, and more–God is always here–even when we are conscious of our failures, our sin, and when everything seems to be going wrong, God does not give up on us.

Each day this seeker continues her search for God. But she has come to realize that God is not a hidden God.

So now–in the morning, when she opens her eyes, she tries to remember as well, to open the treasure, and to hear the words of God speaking softly like a whisper, and, at other times, like a blare of a trumpet. And the words that are spoken by God are; "You are my beloved, my favor rests in you."

So—the search continues—but now it is a different kind of search.

Of course, there may be plenty of reasons to doubt the existence of God. There may be plenty of reasons to give up on God, to give up on the search, and to give up on the people and places where we were told and taught that God would be found. But C.S. Lewis reminds us that 'in the end, searching for God is not a journey of the mind but of the soul."

Gregory of Nyssa states: "Moses' vision of God began with light. Afterwards God spoke to him in a cloud. But when Moses rose higher and became more perfect, he saw God in the darkness."

Life has its moments—its moments of struggle and survival—its moments of joy and grief—its moments of answers with so many questions and questions still in search of answers. And life goes on—each morning we lift our head off the pillow and face the battles of the day. But, does it have to be a battle? A poet once wrote: "Life is not about waiting for the storms to pass—it is about learning how to dance in the rain."

And, does it matter the size of the dance floor? What matters is the size of the heart.

About the Author

Sister Sandra Makowski was born Sandra Ann Makowski and grew up in Binghamton, New York. Six minutes after her birth her twin sister, Carole Jean was born. They shared the same bedroom, clothes, thoughts and ultimately the same vocation. They graduated from high school and entered the Sisters of St. Mary of Namur. They knew the Sisters from grade school, and witnessed the love and kindness that the Sisters had for one another - and they wanted that for themselves. Her sister, Carole, who took the name Sister Jean, was killed in a car accident in 1981 while on her way to serve in the missions. This tragedy changed Sandra's life and she learned the courage of survival and the kindness of friends.

Sister Sandra's first book was published in 2014 and it is titled "The Side of Kindness."

Sister Sandra received a Bachelor's degree in education and went on to receive a Masters degree in religious studies and licentiate in canon law, Along with the knowledge gained from her studies, she writes from her first hand experience as a woman working in the Catholic Church for 42 years as a teacher, canonist, judge, and presently Chancellor for the Diocese of Charleston, S.C. She authored her second book "The Invisible Women."

In"Searching for God and Finding the treasure" she recounts a woman's journey in her search for God and discovering, in this journey, that God is with us in all of our moments of life.

Recovering the Lost Art of Being Kind

The
SIDE
of
KINDNESS

SANDRA MAKOWSKI, SSMN

All too often, the complex society in which we live forces us to take sides—between political parties, religious denominations, sports teams, and more. But how can we be sure we've chosen the right side? And is there a way to overcome the divisiveness and hostility that often accompanies choosing one side over another? This book offers a unique look at choosing the side that really matters: the side of kindness.In a series of sometimes humorous, always thought-provoking reflections, author Sandra Makowski reminds us that we can always choose the side of kindness, even in the smallest decisions of daily life. Our conversation, tone of voice, and even the way we dress can be shaped by kindness. And together, those many small decisions can make a great difference in our broken and fragile world.Sister Sandra was born Sandra Ann Makowski in 1947 in Binghamton, NY. On the same day, just six minutes earlier, her twin sister, Carole Jean was born. They shared the same bedroom, clothes, thoughts, and ultimately the same vocation. They graduated from high school and entered The Sisters of St. Mary of Namur in Buffalo, NY. They knew the Sisters since grade school, and witnessed the love and kindness that the Sisters had for one another – and they wanted that for themselves.Her sister, Carole, who took the religious name of Sister Jean, was killed in a car accident in 1981 while on her way to serve in the missions. The tragedy changed Sandra's life and she learned the courage of survival and the kindness of friends.After receiving a Bachelor's Degree in Education and Master's Degree in Religious Education, she went on to receive a licentiate degree in Canon law from The Catholic University of America. She worked as a canonist in the Buffalo NY and Charleston, SC dioceses. In 2010 she was appointed Chancellor of the diocese of Charleston.